heavenly metal *twisted wire*

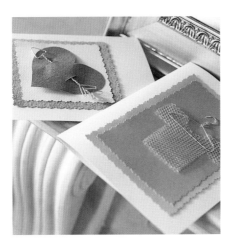

lisa brown

heavenly metal *twisted wire*

create 20 chic and shimmering accents for the home

lisa brown

D&C
David and Charles

A DAVID & CHARLES BOOK
Copyright © David & Charles Limited 2001, 2007

David & Charles is an F+W Publications Inc. company
4700 East Galbraith Road
Cincinnati, OH 45236

First published in the UK in 2007
Text and photographs originally published in 2001 as *Metalcraft*

Text and project designs copyright © Lisa Brown 2001, 2007

Lisa Brown has asserted her right to be identified as author
of this work in accordance with the Copyright, Designs and
Patents Act, 1988.

A catalogue record for this book is available from the
British Library.

ISBN-13: 978-0-7153-2775-3
ISBN-10: 0-7153-2775-5

Senior Editor Jennifer Fox-Proverbs
Desk Editor Bethany Dymond
Design Assistant Eleanor Stafford
Proofreader Joan Gubbin
Photography Lucinda Symons
Step photography Brian Hatton

Printed in China by SNP Leefung Pte Ltd
for David & Charles
Brunel House   Newton Abbot   Devon

Visit our website at www.davidandcharles.co.uk

David & Charles books are available from all good bookshops;
alternatively you can contact our Orderline on 0870 9908222 or
write to us at FREEPOST EX2 110, D&C Direct, Newton Abbot,
TQ12 4ZZ (no stamp required UK only); US customers call
800-289-0963 and Canadian customers call 800-840-5220.

*Working with metal in these projects is straightforward and safe
provided proper precautions are taken. Protective gloves, goggles and
clothing should be worn whenever you are working with the harder
metals and wires. In particular, protective gloves should be worn when
cutting and filing any of these materials. The author and publisher have
made every effort to ensure that all the instructions in the book are
accurate and safe, and therefore cannot accept liability for any resulting
injury, damage or loss to persons or property, however it may arise.*

contents

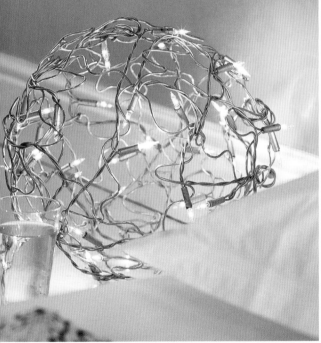

introduction 6

MAGICAL MESH 10
greetings cards 12
celebration cake 16
easter ornaments 20
wire-mesh food covers 24
panelled wardrobe 28

WICKED WIRE 32
wire chandelier 34
curtain-pole finials and holdbacks 40
wire-handled lanterns 44
rusted wire cupboard 50
christmas-light sphere 56

FABULOUS FOIL AND TIN 60
butterfly wind-chimes 62
candy-wrapper mirror frame 66
monogram wreath 70
tin splashback 74

METALCRAFTING 80
materials and equipment 82
techniques 86

templates 92
resources, acknowledgments,
about the author 95
index 96

introduction

Part of my work as a journalist and author for interior design and craft publications has involved coming up with accessible ideas for making useful and beautiful items for the home. In my experience, projects using 'soft' materials such as fabric, paper and trimmings always spring to mind more readily than ideas for harder materials, where the tendency is to steer away from anything that might require too many specialist tools or which appears to be in any way dangerous to work with. For many, metal is one of the most intimidating materials in this category, and anything to do with it is usually avoided before even exploring the possibilities. However, over the years, I have come to realize just how accessible and interesting a material metal is.

I've discovered that there are many easy-to-work-with metals available that are far removed from the wrought iron we normally associate with this material. I've also found the creative potential of metal to be enormous. My first few successful projects then spurred me on to explore more ideas, the result of which is collected in this book.

The discovery of metals marked a fundamental step in the progress of human civilization. Subsequently, our ability, with the help of specific tools such as rolling mills and drawplates, to manipulate metals

Delicate wirework recalls the filigree work of the past.

into sheet and wire form has enabled us to mould it into almost any shape imaginable. This, coupled with the fact that metal can then be cut, twisted, pierced and folded, makes it a most attractive and useful medium with which to work.

Wire can be threaded with beads or wrapped round glass nuggets.

The use of metal sheet and wire goes back thousands of years, and these forms have always been used both for function and for decoration. These days, in the area of craft, metalwork is often associated with such arts as the tinware of Mexico or the wirework of Zimbabwe, both of which utilize cheap, recycled materials. In the West, we have the choice of buying metals from specialist suppliers at relatively low cost or recycling metals for purely decorative purposes.

Three forms of metal are used in this book: foil, wire and wire mesh, the latter being a material that seems to combine the qualities of the first two. Of the finer of the foils, I have explored the use of foil sweet wrappers, an interesting idea for recycling metal. Among the heavier embossing foils are thicker flat metals such as tin (another easily recycled metal) and sheet aluminium, one of the most satisfying flat metals to work with as it is easy to cut, lightweight and very malleable.

Thin sheet metal can be cut and embossed easily.

Loops of wire threaded with beads and fitted between lampshade rings are the basis for a chandelier hung with discs of glass.

The majority of the wires used in this book are readily available, with the exception of a very thick aluminium wire which can be purchased from a specialist supplier by mail order (see Resources). The rest are manufactured for everyday household, gardening and craft use in an enormous range of thicknesses and metal types, providing an interesting choice of colours. As well as being used in its single form, wire can also be adapted to enhance strength, flexibility and decoration by twisting it, a method that has been used in several of the designs.

Wire meshes start with basic chicken wire at one end of the spectrum and work through to the finer meshes, which were developed initially as a sculpting aid. Their moulding and decorative qualities offer huge potential for craft possibilities.

The very thick wires are available from specialist metal suppliers, while the finer foils, wires and meshes can be purchased from craft suppliers and hardware shops (see Resources page 95). All the types of metal mentioned above are fully described in the Metalcrafting section

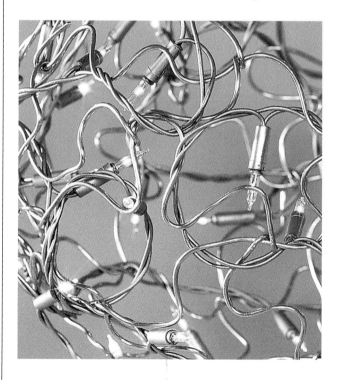

A sculptural light made from flexible wire woven into a sphere and threaded with Christmas lights.

at the back of the book. One of the great things about working with metal is that the materials are relatively inexpensive and can be conveniently purchased in small quantities, even from the specialist suppliers. I have endeavoured to keep the designs throughout the book as accessible as possible, so the majority can be made up using a basic set of tools, with just a few requiring other inexpensive extras, such as tin snips and wire cutters.

There are a range of projects to make, from quirky gifts such as the mesh birthday cake and cards, to a grand chandelier and decorative cupboard. Familiar crafting materials such as beads are also included, and common crafting techniques such as jewellery making, paper embossing and even découpage can be found lurking amongst the metalcraft.

Putting this book together has opened my eyes even further to the possibilities of this fascinating material, through designs and

Wire mesh can be moulded with ease into decorative shapes.

ideas in which metal in its many forms has been transformed into the most delicate and decorative objects, or something strong, stylish and practical. I hope these designs will take away the fear of metal as something that is hard, dangerous and uncompromising to work with, and will be an inspiration to explore the potential of this diverse and exciting material to the full.

Lisa Brown

magical mesh

greetings cards

Metal makes an ordinary gift card

into a unique and longlasting

keepsake. Keep offcuts from larger

projects for last-minute greetings.

Y ou can make greetings cards for different occasions using a combination of the finer silver mesh and jewellery wire. Suggestions are provided here for Valentine's day, Mother's Day and the birth of a new baby, but any occasion deserves a gorgeous handmade card.

materials & equipment

coloured and plain papers

coloured lightweight card (optional)

paper edging scissors

pencil

wire modelling mesh, 5mm (¼in) diamond pattern

heavy-duty scissors

wire-edged ribbon

0.8mm silver-plated jewellery wire

round- and flat-nosed jewellery pliers

ready-scored blank cards and matching envelopes

paper adhesive

strong all-purpose adhesive

ready-made ribbon roses

craft knife

STEP 1

Cut out squares and rectangles of coloured paper or lightweight card using paper edging scissors, to be used as the background for the motifs. Fold a piece of paper, then draw and cut out half a heart shape against the fold. Open this out and use it as a template to cut out the pink heart. Use the same method to cut out a T-shirt shape from plain paper.

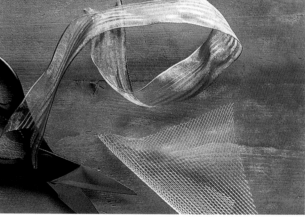

STEP 2

Using heavy-duty scissors, cut a square of wire mesh to act as wrapping for the bouquet design. Fold two opposite corners to the centre and scrunch up the base. Tie it with a bow of wire-edged ribbon, cutting the ends of the bow into a V shape.

STEP 3

Fold a small piece of wire mesh, place the top of the T-shirt template on the fold line and cut around it. Again cutting through both layers of wire mesh, cut out a neck shape on the folded edge.

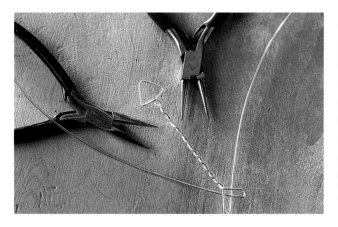

STEP 4

Make an arrow from the silver-plated jewellery wire. Using round-nosed pliers, bend the wire in half and then make a bend at each side to form the arrowhead. Holding both ends of the wire with the flat-nosed pliers and with the arrowhead in your other hand, twist the two ends to make the shaft. Use the round-nosed pliers to bend each end out and then back on itself to make the first pair of feathers.

STEP 5

Twist the ends together for a couple of turns, as before. Repeat this process to the end of the arrow and trim the ends if necessary. Use the same bending and twisting techniques to make the coat hanger. To do this, first bend the triangle, then twist the ends together. Snip off one end close to the twist. Bend the other end to make the curve of the hook and then trim.

STEP 6

Assemble the cards. Use paper adhesive to fix the coloured squares and rectangles in place. Use strong all-purpose adhesive to attach the bouquet wrapper and then the ribbon roses. Slip the hanger inside the mesh T-shirt and use a few small dabs of adhesive to attach these to the card. Using a craft knife, cut slits in the heart large enough to take the arrow. Insert this and glue the heart in place. Fold the cards to complete.

celebration cake

A handmade cake is always well

received, and here is a foolproof

way of providing one that will last

and is guaranteed to delight.

T he cake is simply constructed from one of the stronger versions of the wire mesh often used for sculpting. Decoration is added with a fine wire coil at the top of each tier and a pretty bow to trim the base, while real birthday candles soften the effect.

materials & equipment

pencil

paper

pair of compasses/
round objects

scissors

permanent marker pen

wire modelling mesh,
1cm (⅜in) diamond
pattern

protective gloves

heavy-duty scissors

wire cutters

modelling wire

10 amp fuse wire

tweezers

superglue

0.6mm silver-plated
jewellery wire for coils
(see page 88
for method)

ribbon

birthday cake candles

SAFETY NOTE

Although the mesh is
fine, it is advisable
to wear protective
gloves when handling
cut edges.

STEP 1

Using a pair of compasses or suitable round objects, draw out on paper two circles for the tiers of the cake, the first with a radius of 3.5cm (1⅜in), the second with a radius of 4.5cm (1¾in). Cut out each circle.

STEP 2

Using a permanent marker pen, draw around the two paper circles on to the wire mesh, making each circle slightly larger than its template. Wearing protective gloves, cut out the circles using heavy-duty scissors. Cut a side piece for each tier, each one measuring the length of the circumference of the matching wire mesh circle. Using wire cutters, cut three lengths of modelling wire each measuring the length of the longer side piece, and two lengths each measuring the length of the shorter side piece.

STEP 3

Join the wires into rings the same size as the paper templates. Overlap the ends and bind them with fuse wire. Take a mesh side piece and turn in a small fold along one long edge and then, overlapping the ends, wrap the folded edge around a corresponding wire ring. Do the same with the second side piece and wire ring.

STEP 4

Fit a wire mesh circle over the top of each ring and turn in the edges. Use tweezers to pinch together any pairs of wires along the edge and push them to the inside.

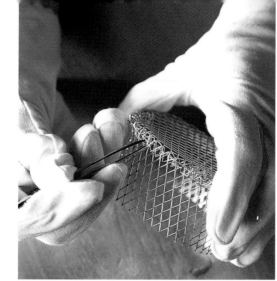

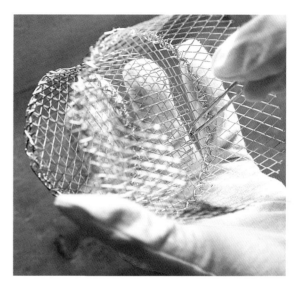

STEP 5

Fit the smaller tier on top of the larger one. Some of the wire mesh along the raw edge of the top tier will cling to the top of the lower tier. Use the tweezers to turn in all the wires neatly.

STEP 6

Superglue the additional rings of modelling wire around the top of each tier. Make two coils of silver-plated jewellery wire the same length as the circumference of the circles. Stretch and flatten the coils, and make into two rings; bind the joins with fuse wire. Glue a ring around the top of each tier. Add the final ring of modelling wire to the base by bending and turning in the lower edge.

SAFETY NOTE
Do not leave lighted candles unattended.

STEP 7

Tie a ribbon bow around the base of the cake. Taper the ends of the birthday cake candles and twist them gently into the mesh of the top tier. Place the cake on a plate before lighting the candles.

easter ornaments

Silvery mesh eggs enclose

pretty, lightweight objects for

gifts, decoration and display.

These delicate objects make an ideal Easter gift – present them individually filled with a feather, blown quail's egg or a silk flower. For decoration, make some to hang from an Easter 'tree' of twisted willow branches sprayed silver. Alternatively, display one on your own mantelpiece or shelf, or suspend it near a window for an eyecatching effect. Each egg is simply constructed from silvery wire mesh, moulded in two halves around an egg shape. These are then joined together, holding a decorative filler of your choice, and finished off with a ribbon.

materials & equipment

eggs for moulds
(use ornamental
plaster or marble
eggs, or hardboiled
hen and duck eggs)

pencil

paper

scissors

wire modelling mesh,
5mm (¼in) diamond
pattern

permanent marker pen

protective gloves

heavy-duty scissors

decorative objects, such
as silk flowers, feathers
and blown quail's eggs

superglue

organza ribbon

fine ribbon or
sewing thread

SAFETY NOTE
Although the mesh is
fine, it is advisable
to wear protective
gloves when handling
cut edges.

STEP 1
Draw an oval shape
on paper, to measure
a little larger than the
egg you are using
as a mould.

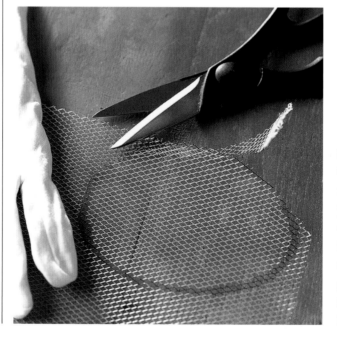

STEP 2
Cut out the egg-shaped
template and use a
permanent marker pen to
draw around the paper
template on to the wire
mesh. Wearing protective
gloves, cut out the shape
from the mesh using
heavy-duty scissors.

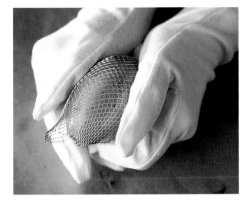

STEP 3
Wearing protective gloves, press, stretch and smooth the wire mesh around the egg, trying not to make tucks at the sides. Slip the mesh off the egg. Make a second shape in the same way.

STEP 4
Still wearing protective gloves, use heavy-duty scissors to trim the irregular edges, to give a neat shape that is slightly larger than half the mould egg.

STEP 5
Overlapping the cut edges and enclosing a decoration, gently press the two mesh halves together. The edges will catch together in places, but secure the join with tiny drops of superglue.

STEP 6
Tie organza ribbon over the join and knot it at the top. Tie a bow and trim the ends with either a diagonal or a V-shaped cut. Use as an ornament, Easter gift or hanging decoration, suspending it with sewing thread or fine ribbon.

wire-mesh food covers

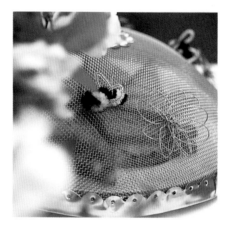

Keep marauding insects away

from your picnic on hot summer

days with these decorative metal

food covers.

These useful food covers are ideal for protecting food and can be used both indoors and out. They are made to fit over a dinner plate and a side plate, so the bowls that are used as a mould must correspond to these sizes. The main part of the cover is made from strong steel mesh, reinforced with an aluminium mesh band and a decorative pewter scalloped border. Skeletal wire flowers decorate the mesh expanse and charming bees, made from pipe cleaners, either sit on the mesh or 'fly' around it suspended from a length of wire.

materials & equipment

large and small bowls, for moulds

fabric tape measure

fine stainless steel wire mesh

permanent marker pen

protective gloves

scissors

pliers

aluminium or other pliable mesh

fine fuse wire

thin card

pewter sheet

revolving hole punch

high-tack, fast-drying adhesive, suitable for metal

1.5mm galvanized wire

black and yellow pipe cleaners

small beads

large bead (with hole large enough to take two lengths of wire), for handle

STEP 1

Turn the bowl to be used as a mould upside down and measure from one side of the rim, over the top, to the opposite side. Add 4cm (1½in) to this measurement and draw a circular template to this diameter. Use the template as a guide to cut out a circle from stainless steel wire mesh, wearing protective gloves. Start to form the mesh circle over the bowl, bending the edges under the rim of the bowl. Continue gently pressing and bending the mesh until it forms close contact with the bowl and the edges are bent over the rim neatly.

STEP 2

Pull the mesh off the bowl by unhooking the edges. Bend back the edges using pliers and trim to create a neat edge. Push the mesh back into shape if necessary. Cut a strip of aluminium mesh (or any very pliable mesh) 1.5cm (½in) wide and long enough to fit around the rim of the bowl. Join lengths if necessary by wiring the ends together. Lay the strip in position and stitch fuse wire through both layers of mesh all the way around to join.

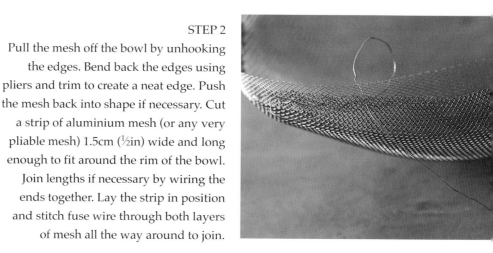

STEP 3

Use the scalloped edge shape on page 92 to make a template. Allow 2.5cm (1in) to fold into the bowl. Lay this on the pewter sheet, draw around it using the permanent marker and cut out the required length of edging using scissors. Make a hole in each scallop using a revolving hole punch.

STEP 4

Mark the fold line along the pewter strip and carefully bend it over. Apply adhesive to the inside of the strip and stick it in position all around the rim of the bowl shape, smoothing out any folds in the pewter as you go.

STEP 5

Cut a piece of galvanized wire about 70cm (28in) long. Wrap it around your index and middle fingers, making about 12 loops. Remove the loops from your hand and thread a length of wire through the bottom of all the loops. Twist the ends of the wire together and pull the loops to form a flower shape. Wrap the wire around the centre of the flower a few times and leave a stem about 5cm (2in) long at the back.

STEP 7

Trace the scalloped circle template on page 92, then use to make a card template with a scalloped edge. Lay this on the pewter sheet, draw around it using the marker pen and cut out the scalloped top using scissors. Make a hole in each scallop shape using the revolving hole punch. Make a hole in the centre of the top and glue it in position. Push one end of a piece of wire through the hole in a large bead and thread small beads on to this. When the loop is the required size, push the other end of the wire through the large bead and twist to secure. Push this through the top of the food cover, open out the ends of the wire and glue in place. Thread, loop and secure the flower and bee stems through the wire mesh.

STEP 6

Cut a piece of black pipe cleaner to make the bee's body. Cut a piece of galvanized wire about 25cm (10in) long and make an antenna shape at one end. Wrap the wire around the bee's body and start to form a wing shape. Thread the beads on to the wire. When the wing is the required size, bend the wire under the bee's body and back up to form the second wing. Again thread beads on to it and bend the wire to form the second antenna, trimming the end if necessary. Wrap a short length of yellow pipe cleaner around the bee to make the stripes. Twist a piece of wire around the bee to form a stem.

panelled wardrobe

The honeycombed effect of chicken

wire brings a decorative element

and a Swedish country-look to an

old wardrobe.

Chicken wire is traditionally used for outdoor fencing, but over the years it has also been brought into the home. It has most commonly appeared in kitchens, used to adapt a cupboard into an airy and scavenger-free larder. Latterly, chicken wire has been used once again in a practical as well as decorative way for lining cupboard doors, this time for the storage of linen and glassware. Fabric is often placed behind the chicken wire, adding an extra dimension of colour and texture.

materials & equipment

junk wardrobe
sandpaper
white oil-based paint
paintbrush
screwdriver
jigsaw (if solid panels)
rag
protective gloves
protective goggles
wire cutters
chicken wire, for panels
staple gun
gingham fabric, for panel curtains
needle, pins and sewing thread
expanding curtain wire
screw eyes and hooks

SAFETY NOTE
Wire can be sharp, so always wear goggles to protect your eyes.

STEP 1
Sand all the woodwork ready for painting, then apply two coats of white oil-based paint, allowing each coat to dry before applying the next. Unscrew each door from its hinges and lay it face down. Carefully prize off the hardboard panels and remove the mirrors (if any, as in the cupboard shown here). If your doors have solid panels, cut these out using a jigsaw. Wipe away any dirt or dust that may have gathered in the recess.

STEP 2
Wearing protective gloves and goggles, and using wire cutters, cut a chicken wire panel for each door, making it slightly larger than the door panel. Cut as close to the honeycomb shape as possible to avoid leaving any sharp wire ends.

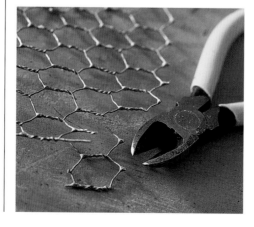

STEP 3
Still wearing protective gloves, snip out a small square from each corner of the chicken wire panel, so that it can be fitted neatly inside the recess.

STEP 4
Press the chicken wire gently into the recess, moulding the edges with your hands. Use a staple gun to secure the edges of the wire in place.

STEP 5
Cut a fabric panel for each door, 12cm (5in) longer than the panel and twice the width. Stitch a narrow double hem down each side and a casing 2cm (¾in) deep across the top and bottom edges.

STEP 6
Cut four lengths of expanding curtain wire, each about 2cm (¾in) wider than the panel. Screw a small eye into the end of each wire. Thread the wires though the casings of each fabric panel, gathering up the fabric slightly as you go.

This idea translates well for a kitchen cupboard. Dispense with the fabric and spray the chicken wire white for an easy-to-clean and attractive door front.

STEP 7
Screw the small hooks into the back of the door on either side of the chicken wire panels at top and bottom, then attach the fabric panels so that they hang quite taut.

wicked wire

wire chandelier

Curled wire and glittering beads

make an irresistible combination,

shown off to great decorative

effect in this modern update of a

luxurious French-style chandelier.

Traditional metal lamp rings are used to make up the top and bottom of the chandelier, anchoring the design together. Between these sit strong wire shapes threaded with pretty beads and embellished with curls. The beads have been chosen for their complementary shades and eyecatching combination of styles including matt, foiled and faceted. A scalloped wire fringe, threaded with beads, is fixed around the bottom ring. For extra decoration, and to shield the eyes from the glare of the bulb, glass discs are frosted and hung between the wire shapes.

materials & equipment

12 pre-drilled
glass shapes

etching spray

newspaper

20cm (8in) and
12cm (5in) diameter
metal lamp rings

silver metallic spray paint

2mm and 1.5mm
galvanized wire

0.6mm silver-plated
jewellery wire

pliers

assorted glass beads

round-nosed pliers

24 small earring hooks

small jewellery pliers

6 small split rings

SAFETY NOTE
Wire can be sharp, so always wear goggles to protect your eyes.

STEP 1
Apply etching spray to both sides of the glass shapes. In a well-ventilated area, lay the discs on newspaper and then cover with spray following the manufacturer's instructions. Allow the first side to dry before turning over and spraying the other side. Spray the two metal lamp rings with silver metallic paint to match the galvanized and jewellery wires, again working on newspaper in a well-ventilated area.

STEP 2
Wearing protective goggles, cut six 70cm (28in) lengths of 2mm galvanized wire and bend each in half to form the template shape (A) on page 94.

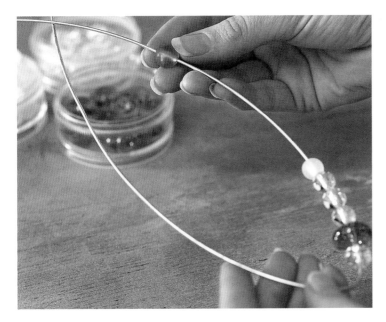

STEP 3

Thread the wire with an assortment of glass beads, in the same chosen pattern and colour scheme on both halves of the shaped wire.

STEP 4

Use round-nosed pliers to bend the ends of the wire into curls to match the template shape (B) on page 94.

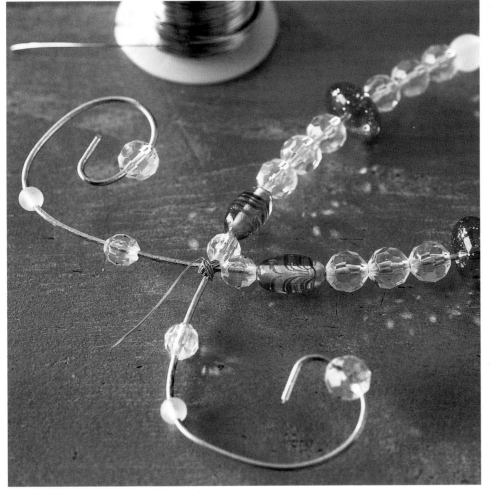

STEP 5

Cross the wire over at the point shown on the template, arranging your design of beads so that some are above the cross-over point. Bind tightly with jewellery wire at this point to secure the shape. Repeat steps 3, 4 and 5 for the other five lengths of wire.

STEP 6
Use the jewellery wire to bind the first shaped piece to the large lamp ring. Bind at the top of each curl, then continue around the ring to bind the next shaped piece in position, and so on until all six pieces are attached.

STEP 7
Use the jewellery wire to bind the bottom point of each shaped piece to the small lamp ring, using the same binding method as in step 6. Stretch or compress the shapes to fit exactly.

STEP 8
Using jewellery wire, make loops to achieve a scalloped effect around the lower ring. Bind the initial piece of jewellery wire to the bottom point of one of the shapes. Thread with a chosen pattern of beads and bind to the bottom point of the adjacent shape to form a loop about 4cm (1½in) deep. Continue binding in this way until all six loops are in position.

STEP 9

Using the 1.5mm galvanized wire, make six small pendant droppers to hang from the lower ring between each loop. For each dropper, take a 6cm (2½in) length of wire and bend a tiny loop in one end. Thread with your chosen pattern of beads, then make another small loop in the other end and attach to a small earring hook. Attach the dropper to the lower ring at the bottom point of the shape by hooking in place with the earring hook and squeezing closed with small jewellery pliers to secure.

STEP 10

Make six larger droppers to suspend from the cross-over points of the main wire shapes. Make each dropper following the method in step 9 but with a 10cm (4in) length of wire, and this time attach a small earring hook to both ends. Suspend a frosted glass shape from one earring hook and use the other earring hook to suspend the dropper from the cross-over point. Attach earring hooks to the final six frosted glass shapes and hang from a split ring positioned around the central point of the wire curls.

curtain-pole finials and holdbacks

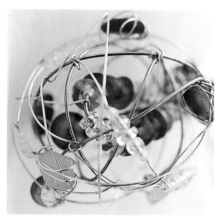

Tangled silver wire and glittering

beads in turquoise and white

combine to make up these unusual

finials and holdbacks.

These sculptural spheres are designed to sit decoratively on the ends of a ready-made silver curtain pole and matching holdbacks. The tangled wire ball is made from a frame of strong galvanized wire reinforced with silver jewellery wire. To introduce colour and light, the wires are threaded with a combination of beads and wrapped around frosted glass nuggets. The light, translucent style of these spheres works particularly well with simple white voile curtains that act to diffuse the light.

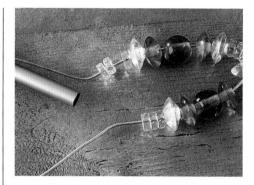

STEP 1

Using pliers, and wearing protective goggles, cut a 25cm (10in) length of 2mm galvanized wire and bend it in half. Thread with large-holed glass beads in your chosen pattern on both halves of the bent wire, then bend the ends of the wire at a slight angle to form 'tails'. Push the tails into one end of the hollow metal curtain pole.

STEP 2

Cut another piece of galvanized wire about 1m (40in) long, tuck one end down into the hollow pole and then wind the wire around the central bead loop in a random fashion to form a loose cage. Tuck the remaining end into the pole as before to secure.

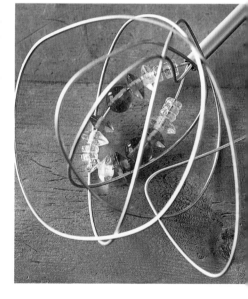

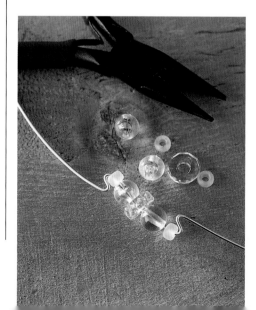

STEP 3

Cut a 1m (40in) length of jewellery wire and thread with a few small beads about 10cm (4in) from one end. Using small jewellery pliers, bend a small kink in the wire on either side of the beads to keep them in place.

STEP 4

Start weaving in the length of jewellery wire, using it to bind the cross-over points of the galvanized wire cage to hold it securely in place. Thread this wire with more beads, kinking it as before, and then continue to bind the cage. Finish the ends of the wire by winding tightly around the wire of the original cage. Use another piece of beaded wire if necessary to finish the binding so that the cage feels firm.

STEP 5

Cut a 1m (40in) length of jewellery wire and about 10cm (4in) from one end wind a length of the wire securely around a glass nugget in two or three directions, as shown.

STEP 6

Wind the jewellery wire around the wire cage as before, adding more nuggets as you go. Finish the ends of the jewellery wire by winding tightly around the wire of the original cage. Repeat steps 1–6 to make up the other finial.

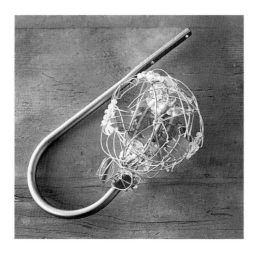

STEP 7

For the holdback, make a beaded and bound cage as for the finial but a little smaller. Using jewellery wire, bind the central tails 7cm (2¾in) in from the end of the holdback, then bind a few glass nuggets around this to hide the bound wires.

wire-handled lanterns

These charming outdoor lanterns

are made from old jars, wire and

beads, and look pretty whether

or not the candles are lit.

M ade from the most basic of materials, these pretty lanterns will grace the garden or an outdoor dining table. They work equally well hung from a hook, nestled in a tree or free-standing on steps or a tabletop. Different effects can be achieved by choosing a variety of glass jars, from the antique pharmaceutical type to an everyday jam jar. A range of wires can be used, from glamorous silver-plated jewellery wire to rustic florist's wire, and the same goes for the beads. Each lantern contains a candle stabilized with fine sand.

materials & equipment

0.6mm silver-plated
jewellery wire

wire cutters

protective goggles

old glass jars

ruler or tape measure

small pliers

high-gloss silver beads
(with holes large
enough to take two
lengths of wire)

lengths of florist's wire

oval beads

SAFETY NOTE
Wire can be sharp, so
always wear goggles
to protect your eyes.

STEP 1
For the beaded-net design, use wire cutters to cut 16 lengths of jewellery wire to measure one-and-a-half times the height of your chosen jar. Using the small pliers, curve over one end of each of the lengths of wire.

STEP 2
Group the lengths of wire into eight pairs, then join each pair together with a single high gloss bead, as shown. To prevent the beads from sliding, bend each piece of wire outwards.

STEP 3
Take two beaded pairs and join them together by sliding a bead on to one wire from each pair, about 3cm (1¼in) down from the top beads. Keep a ruler handy to check this measurement. Again, bend the wire outwards to prevent the bead from sliding.

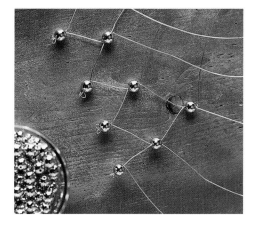

STEP 4

Repeat step 3 with more pieces of wire
and more beads, until all the pieces of wire
are linked together. Add a third row of
beads using the same method.

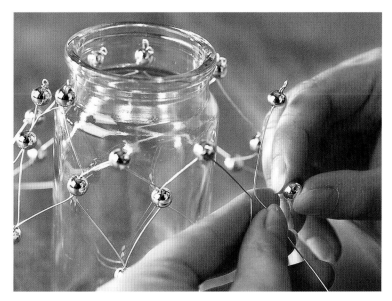

STEP 5

Wrap your flexible net of
beaded wire around the body
of the jar and, taking up the
loose ends along each vertical
edge, join them with more
beads using the method given
in step 3, to form a seamless
net enclosing the jar.

STEP 6

To attach the top of the wire net and provide a handle, cut a length of
wire five times the height of the jar. Wrap the wire around the neck of
the jar and secure one end by twisting it to itself to make a collar. Leave
the other end dangling. With the pliers, take the little hooks at the top of
the net and hook each one over the top of the wire collar. Take the
dangling length of wire to the opposite side of the jar and at its half-
way point thread it under the collar. Bring it back to its starting point by
winding it back around the single-strand handle to strengthen. Twist a
heart shape at the top of the handle. Tighten any slack in the wire collar
by twisting it with the pliers. Cut off the surplus ends with wire cutters.

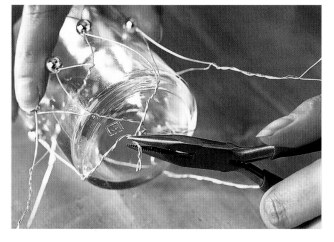

STEP 7

To finish the base of the design, place the loose ends
of the wire into pairs as before and twist them from
the point at the base of the jar. Then take each twisted
section and join it underneath the jar to another
twisted section on the opposite side of the jar.
Continue until all the wires have been joined, then
cut off any surplus wire using wire cutters.

STEP 8

For the wire-spiral design, take eight lengths of florist's wire and use small pliers to curl one end of each length around to make a spiral shape (see page 89). Take the other end and twist a spiral in the opposite direction.

STEP 9

Using wire cutters, cut a piece of florist's wire approximately three times as long as the bead. Using the small pliers, curl one end of it, hook it on to a spiral and pinch it together. Thread the bead on to the wire, then cut off some surplus wire but leave just enough to make another hook to attach to another spiral. Link the spirals together in this way to make a collar for the jar. This jar had two collars, using four spirals per collar. Slide each collar on to the jar. Small circumference adjustments can be made to hold the collar in place by tightening or loosening the spirals. For larger or smaller jars, vary the number of spirals.

STEP 10

Twist a single length of florist's wire around the neck of the jar and secure. Cut off the surplus wire using wire cutters. Using the small pliers, hook a length of wire inside the collar on one side and another on the other side of the collar. Thread a bead on to each and twist the wire at the top to make a handle. Using the small pliers, spiral the tips to finish.

A paperweight or doorstop can be made using the same method as the beaded net jar. Replace the glass jar with stones and use a length of 1mm galvanized wire.

rusted wire cupboard

Reminiscent of antique French

wirework, this cupboard is made

from a combination of chicken

wire and rust-effect twisted wire.

This pretty cupboard was inspired by a French antique version made from twisted wire which had been left to rust, adding to its charm. The body is made up from basic chicken wire, which is then reinforced with a twisted wire frame at the front and back. The excess wire on the frame and door is used to make decorative spirals at the front. Further decoration is added in the form of a flattened coil loop. Here, iron wire (left outside for a couple of days to rust) has been used both to aid strength and flexibility, and finally to bind everything in place.

materials & equipment

block of 25mm (1in) MDF (medium-density fiberboard), 29 x 22cm (11½ x 8¾in)

piece of small-gauge chicken wire, 60cm (24in) square

protective gloves

protective goggles

wire cutters

bent-nosed pliers

hammer

4 lengths of 0.5mm rusted iron wire, twisted together to approx 6m (20ft) (see page 90 for method)

2 lengths of 0.5mm rusted iron wire, twisted together to approx 3m (10ft) (see page 90 for method)

length of untwisted 0.5mm rusted iron wire, approx 3m (10ft), for binding

wooden spoon

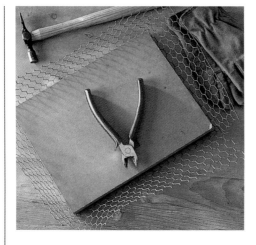

STEP 1
Lay the MDF block on the chicken wire. Wearing protective gloves and goggles, use wire cutters to cut the wire. Leave a 9cm (3½in) margin all round (cut as close to the honeycomb shapes as possible to avoid leaving sharp ends). Cut out a square at each corner, leaving 1cm (½in) overlapping the length of each side. Bend up the sides at right angles to the block of wood, using your hands and a hammer, to create a sharp right-angled bend.

STEP 2
Remove the block of wood and join the corners by bending over the extra 1cm (⅜in). Secure by weaving through, folding back and cutting off any excess wire.

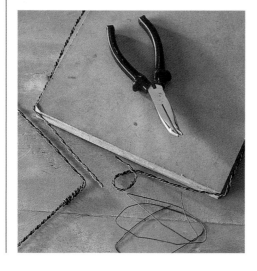

STEP 3
Cut a 110cm (44in) length of thicker twisted wire. Bend it around the block using bent-nosed pliers to make sharp right-angled corners. Remove from the block and join the ends with the binding wire. Trim the excess wire and lay aside. Cut another piece of thicker twisted wire 115cm (46in) long, bend it evenly around the block of wood and remove. With the two equal lengths at the top, make a loop with one length for hanging. Join it to the other length using binding wire and binding on either side of the loop.

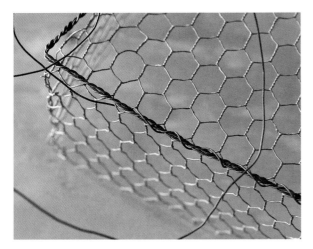

STEP 4
Place the back wire rectangle (with the hanging loop) on to the back of the chicken wire box and wire it into place tightly with binding wire.

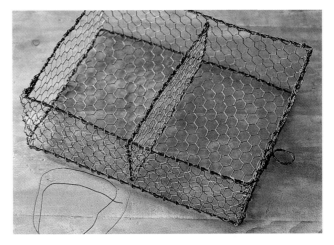

STEP 5
Attach the front rectangle in the same way; you will need to tuck under any protruding cut sections of the chicken wire. Make a shelf in the same manner, first measuring the internal space into which it will fit. Wearing protective gloves, cut the shelf from the chicken wire. Frame with a length of thicker twisted wire and fix it in place with binding wire.

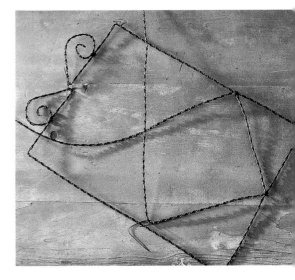

STEP 6
To make the door, take a piece of the thicker twisted wire 150cm (60in) long and bend it around the block, leaving equal ends at the top. Bend each one back on itself at the middle, remove from the block of wood and create the spirals as shown. Bind each one to the horizontal edge beneath it and bind the centre together temporarily.

STEP 7
Take another length of the thicker twisted wire and, with the binding wire, attach the centre of the length, which has been bent at a right angle, to the centre of the base of the door. Bring the two sides up and attach them in the same manner one-third of the way up the sides. Repeat two-thirds of the way up the sides as shown, and bring the two ends to meet between the loosely joined central horizontals beneath.

STEP 8
Undo the loose wire and tightly bind the four lengths together in a line. Turn the two ends into spirals as shown and bind together where they meet the original pair on either side and where they meet each other.

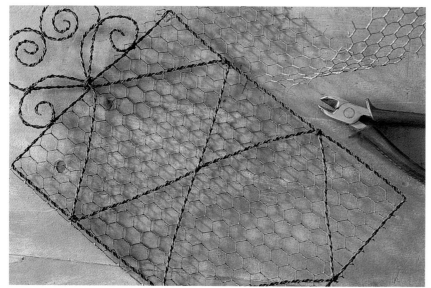

STEP 9
Lay the door on a piece of chicken wire and, wearing protective gloves, cut out the wire to fit.

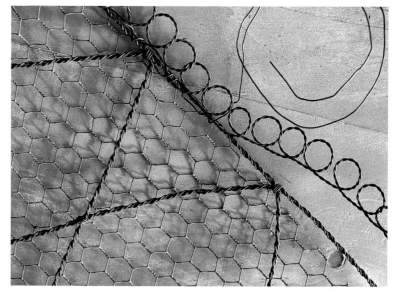

STEP 10
Take the 3m (10ft) length of thinner twisted wire and wind it around the handle of a wooden spoon to make a long coil. Pull the wire off the handle and flatten the loops (see page 88 for method), then bind it on to the door edge, securing the chicken wire at the same time.

STEP 11

Make two simple hinges by binding the right side of the door to the box frame, in two evenly spaced places. Do not bind too tightly, to allow the door to be opened easily.

Decorative spirals are made from twisted rusted wire bound together for strength with single lengths of wire.

christmas-light sphere

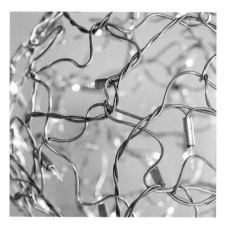

This magical wire sphere threaded

with Christmas lights casts

an ambient glow that is ideal

for bedrooms.

ire sculpted into interesting shapes is infiltrating the top end of the lighting market. Christmas lights are also becoming popular, with an array of styles and colours available. This unusual sphere encompasses both these elements in a lightweight sculpture that looks good whether lit or unlit. It is made from thick aluminium wire, which is surprisingly easy to work with. The wire is worked from one continuous length to aid strength, but if you run out more lengths can be added.

materials & equipment

3.25mm aluminium wire (usually sold by weight, you will need approximately 250g/8oz)

wire cutters

bent-nosed pliers

20 or 24 bulb Christmas lights

silver spray paint

masking tape

STEP 1

Using the wire from the roll, begin to crinkle it with your hands in a wiggly fashion, continuing until you have enough to form a circle with a diameter of about 40cm (16in).

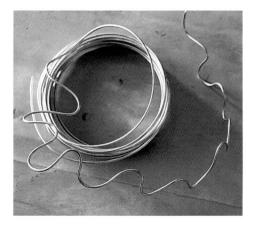

STEP 2

Join the circle by twisting the beginning of the wire around at this point and then continue to make a similar circle at right angles to the first.

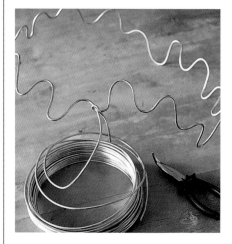

STEP 3

Bring the wire around again and twist to secure around the original circle, tightening with bent-nosed pliers if necessary, then again begin a new crinkly circle.

STEP 4

When the third circle is complete and secured in the same way as before, alter direction and make your new circles horizontally, this time twisting the wire each time it crosses another. You will need to wind your roll of wire into a tighter roll so that it passes more easily through gaps in the 'weave'.

STEP 5

Continue in this manner until the sphere resembles an orderly tangle. You can easily adjust the form at this stage, pushing and pulling it into a spherical shape.

STEP 6

Mask each Christmas-light bulb with masking tape. Making sure the bulbs are not plugged in, spray the flex silver, then leave to dry. Remove the masking tape. Push and thread the Christmas lights through the sphere, wrapping them around the wire so that they are evenly spaced. This is quite time consuming, as you need to take the full Christmas light length in and out of the ball; wrap it into as small a roll as possible to enable you to do this more easily.

fabulous
foil and tin

butterfly wind-chimes

Transform ordinary wind chimes with light-catching aluminium and bead butterflies suspended from twisted wire stems. The delicate finished effect means that the design would look just as good inside the home as it does outside.

Stone and water features are commonly used in the garden, but bright metal – particularly aluminium, with its rust-free qualities – is an ideal material for something a bit more sculptural. Here ready-made wind chimes are customized with ornamental butterflies cut from sheet aluminium, then given a three-dimensional effect with a dotted design on the wings and body using a tracing wheel and moulded shape. Beads maximize the light-catching effect, and the butterflies are suspended on twisted wire as though they are flying.

materials & equipment

piece of 36 gauge (0.2mm) sheet aluminium, 25 x 40cm (10 x 16in)

ballpoint pen

scissors

tracing wheel

small hole punch

wooden spoon

2 lengths of 1.2mm galvanized wire, twisted together to approx 2m (80in) (see page 90 for method)

wire cutters

protective goggles

assorted coloured beads with holes large enough to take twisted wire

strong adhesive

bent-nosed pliers

medium-sized wind chimes

drill with small bit

STEP 1
Trace the butterfly template on page 92. Lay it on the aluminium sheet, hold it in place and draw around it with a ballpoint pen, making an impression on the metal. Repeat to make three more butterflies.

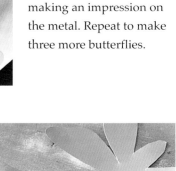

STEP 2
Cut out the butterflies carefully using scissors, cutting between the two wings right up to the body.

STEP 3
Use a tracing wheel to mark all around the outside of the body and the wings, marking horizontal lines across the body as shown.

STEP 4
Mark similar lines where the wings meet the body and a starred circle on each wing, as shown. Use a hole punch to make holes in each of these circles and on the head and base of the body.

SAFETY NOTE
Wire can be sharp, so always wear goggles to protect your eyes.

STEP 5
Bend the body section around the handle of a wooden spoon and flex the wings to create a more three-dimensional effect.

STEP 6
Cut a piece of twisted wire 1m (40in) long and thread it through the holes on the body and head, allowing approximately 6cm (2½in) to protrude at the head end. Thread a single bead on to the wire at this point and add three contrasting beads at the base of the butterfly. You may need to secure them with a dab of strong adhesive. Repeat with another 1m (40in) of twisted wire and a butterfly.

STEP 7
At the head end of the butterflies, open up the twisted wire using bent-nosed pliers and turn each side into a spiral to serve as antennae.

STEP 8
Using a drill, make four holes in a square formation in the wooden disc at the top of the wind chimes. Thread the wire with the butterfly attached through one hole and back up through the opposite hole. Attach the beads and another butterfly to this other end in the same way as in step 6. Open up the antennae as before. Repeat the process with the remaining length of twisted wire and pair of butterflies, threading it through the other two holes.

candy-wrapper mirror frame

Decorate a plain mirror with plain

and patterned candy wrappers in

complementary shades to suit your

bathroom colour scheme.

F oil candy wrappers are a wonderful source of material for brightly coloured, decorative découpage. Here they are used on a mirror, their colours carefully chosen to suit a scheme in the bathroom, comprising purple, mauve, turquoise, green and silver. Some wrappers are plain and some have pretty motifs which add interest to the overall look. The success of the design relies on the wrappers being positioned in a 'contrived randomness', where no two similar colours sit exactly next to each other, and there is a balance of colour over the whole frame. When complete, the frame is varnished for extra protection.

materials & equipment

circular frame of MDF (medium-density fiberboard), cut to preferred size – frame shown measures 55cm (22in) diameter for outer circle and 25cm (10in) for inner circle

metal ruler

pencil

foil sweet wrappers

scissors

glue stick

shellac

paintbrush

mirror square, slightly wider than central hole of frame

4 mirror corner brackets and screws

screwdriver

2 strong D-shaped rings and screws

heavy-duty picture wire

STEP 1
Using a pencil and metal ruler, mark out 6cm (2½in) divisions down the frame of the mirror. This gives you a guide for placing the sweet wrappers and is especially helpful if the wrappers you are using have a right-way-up design. Follow the pencil lines down the outer edge of the mirror frame and mark corresponding lines on to the back for horizontal hanging purposes.

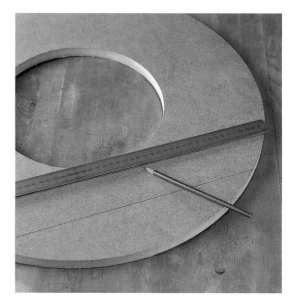

STEP 2
After removing the chocolates (put them in the fridge and don't eat them all at once!) and carefully flattening the wrappers with your fingers, cut the wrappers into different-sized squares and rectangles to allow enough visual variation across the frame.

STEP 3
Rub the glue straight on to the base frame, covering one pencilled section at a time. Stick down the wrappers, gluing and overlapping them at the edges. The design looks balanced when similar styles and colours crop up at regular intervals.

STEP 4
Continue gluing all the wrappers along the pencilled sections and then carry on down both the inside and outside edges of the frame. Loose corners can be glued to the back of the frame.

STEP 5
Apply two coats of shellac to protect the surface. Allow to dry between coats.

STEP 6
Turn the frame over. Using the pencil lines as your guide, position the mirror and screw the corners to the frame. Attach the two D-shaped rings along a pencil line about one-third of the way down from the top of the frame. Secure the picture wire to the two rings.

monogram wreath

Mark your home in style with

a pretty monogrammed wreath

made from silvery aluminium

sheet and galvanized wire.

M onograms provide an elegant source of decoration in the home. They are used in many ways, particularly in soft furnishings and stationery. Here a monogram is introduced in the shape of a wreath, which can be placed outdoors – an unusual way of marking your residence or garden shed – or indoors to grace a mantelpiece or shelf. The aluminium sheet and galvanized wire that it is made from are both weather resistant in that they don't rust. An alphabet is provided on page 93 from which to choose your individual monogram.

materials & equipment

2 lengths of 1.5mm galvanized wire, twisted together to approx 95cm (38in) (see page 90 for method)

0.5mm galvanized wire

wire cutters

bent-nosed pliers

piece of 24 gauge (0.5mm) sheet aluminium, 60 x 30cm (24 x 12in)

masking tape

permanent marker pen

scissors

wire brush

tracing wheel

telephone directory

epoxy resin adhesive, suitable for metal

clothes pegs

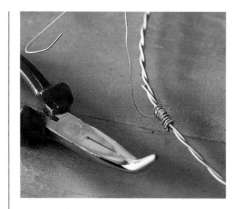

STEP 1

Bend the twisted wire into a circle with a diameter of approximately 29cm (11½in), overlapping 2cm (¾in) where the two ends meet. Bind together tightly to secure with the finer wire.

STEP 2

Make a paper template of a letter and leaf (see page 93). Choose your letter from the alphabet and enlarge it on a photocopier – the letter should be slightly larger than the wire circle in places so that it can be stuck to the circle. Attach the paper templates to the unprotected side of the sheet aluminium (one side is protected with blue film) with masking tape and draw carefully around the shapes with a permanent marker pen.

STEP 3

Remove the paper templates and cut out the shapes using scissors. It may help to change to smaller scissors when cutting around internal curves. Repeat to make as many leaves as you need.

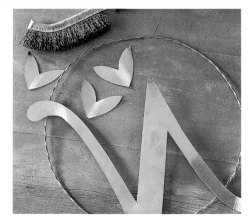

STEP 4
Using the wire brush and working on the back of the metal, brush the centre base of the leaves where they will adhere to the wire circle. Place the letter on to the circle in the desired position and, as with the leaves, abrade the areas where it contacts the wire.

STEP 5
Working on the back of the metal and resting on a telephone directory, push the tracing wheel up the centre of each leaf. Turn the leaves over (blue side) and make a central line between the two leaves to create a three-dimensional effect.

STEP 6
Mix the adhesive according to the manufacturer's instructions (you can use a small piece of metal as a palette and another as a spatula). Put a small quantity on the letter (shiny side) where it has been wire-brushed and immediately secure it in place with a clothes peg until the adhesive sets.

STEP 7
Stick the leaves in place in the same manner, adjusting the position of each one and securing with a clothes peg until the adhesive is firmly set.

STEP 8
Allow the adhesive to dry for the specified time before turning over the wreath. Pull off the protective blue plastic film.

tin splashback

Colourful cans flattened and

framed with scalloped foil

make charming decorations on

a simple tin splashback.

Tiles are the obvious choice for a sink splashback and increasingly, in modern kitchens, stainless steel panels are used, although they are prone to water staining. As a special surface is needed in this area, choose something a little different. This splashback is made from a foil-covered sheet of MDF, decorated with 'pictures' cut from decorative tin cans. Each picture is framed with a contrasting brass foil edge. The overall look is Mediterranean, due mainly to the strong cobalt-blue units, enhanced by the tin can panels depicting exotic contents.

materials & equipment

piece of 12mm (½in) exterior grade MDF (medium-density fiberboard), to fit above sink

yacht varnish (spar varnish)

paintbrush

length of 42 gauge (0.1mm) aluminium foil, to cover MDF

pencil

scissors

short panel pins

hammer

printed tin cans, clean and dry with lids removed

tin opener

protective gloves

tin shears

hide mallet

ruler

36 gauge (0.1mm) brass foil, for trim

small coin

ballpoint pen (optional)

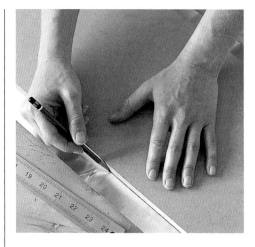

STEP 1

Seal the MDF (medium-density fiberboard) panel with two coats of yacht varnish (spar varnish). Place the panel on the aluminium foil. Mark the position of the MDF, allowing enough room to overlap the edges. Trim the foil to size with scissors.

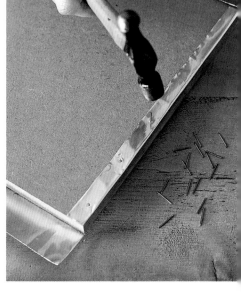

STEP 2

Replace the panel on the foil and fold the metal over the edges. Snip a square of foil from each corner so that you can fold it neatly. Attach the foil to the MDF panel using a hammer and short panel pins.

STEP 3

Remove the bases from the tin cans using a tin opener. Wearing protective gloves, use tin shears to cut open the cans along the side seam.

STEP 4
Neatly cut away the rolled lip at the top and bottom of the cans. Trim off any small spurs of metal and dispose of them carefully.

STEP 5
Place the cans on a flat surface and hammer the metal flat using a hide mallet.

STEP 6
Decide on the size you want your picture squares to be, then measure and trim down the metal cans, making sure you remove any sharp spurs as you cut.

STEP 7
Place the metal squares at equal distances along the splashback, allowing enough room around each for the brass trim. Attach the squares to the splashback along their edges with panel pins.

STEP 8
To make the trim, cut strips of brass foil 2cm (¾in) wide. Draw a line 3mm (⅛in) in from the top edge of each strip. Draw around half of a small coin on to the foil, to make a scalloped edge.

STEP 9
Cut out the scalloped trims using scissors. If desired, draw a simple pattern on to the back of the foil with a ballpoint pen to emboss the metal; otherwise, leave plain.

STEP 10

Place the trims around the tin squares, covering the cut edges of the metal. Attach the trims to the splashback with panel pins hammered in at the base of each scallop join and at the top centre of each scallop.

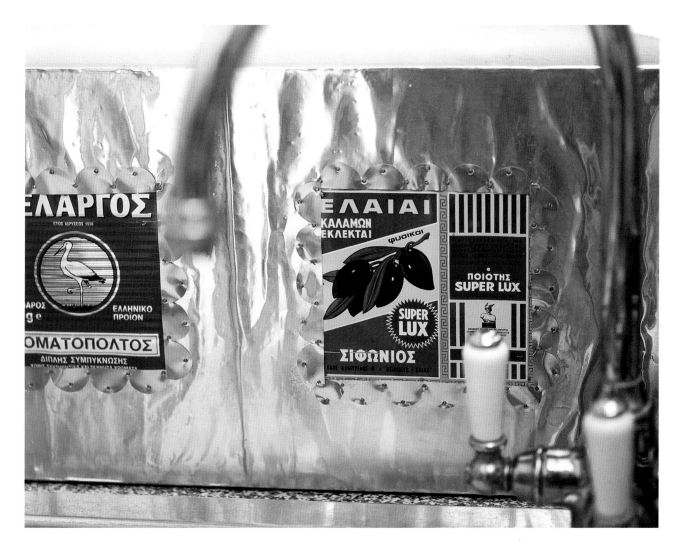

Scour delicatessens for brightly coloured decorative tins – olive and tomato tins from Greece and Spain often have the prettiest designs.

metalcrafting

materials and equipment

MATERIALS

The majority of the materials used in this book are readily available from hardware, craft, art and jewellery suppliers. Some of the thicker sheet metals and wires are only available from specialist suppliers. With the exception of the sheet metals and hardware companies, most suppliers operate a mail order service.

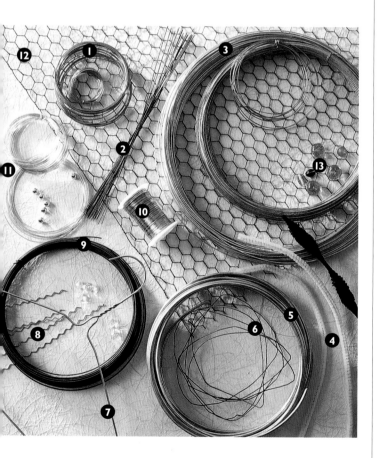

WIRE

Wire is made of solid metal which has the same cross section throughout and can range in thickness from a fine thread to a flexible rod. We most often think of it as having a circular cross section, but it can come in the form of a square or half-round, for example. In simple terms, wire is made by drawing rods of metal through different-sized holes in a drawplate to create wires of different diameters.

Wire can be measured by its diameter in millimetres and/or by a gauge. Confusingly, there are quite a few different standards for wire gauges, varying from country to country. In this book, wire has been supplied in millimetres.

1 SOFT COPPER WIRE
Pliable wire with an attractive and decorative pinkish tone. Available in a variety of gauges from hardware stores and craft suppliers.

2 FLORIST'S WIRE
Dull grey aluminium wire which is very pliable and easy to work with. Available from florist suppliers in pre-cut lengths.

3 GALVANIZED WIRE
Steel wire with a zinc coat to protect it from rusting, making it ideal for outdoor use. This wire is hard and springy, so care should be taken when using it. Available in a variety of gauges from hardware stores.

4 PIPE CLEANERS
These fibre-coated strips of wire come in a range of colours and shapes and add interest to wire projects. Available from craft suppliers.

5 ALUMINIUM WIRE
This matt silver wire is soft, malleable and easy to work with. Finer gauges are available from craft

suppliers. The thicker variety used for the Christmas-light sphere on pages 56–9 is available by mail order from specialist wire suppliers (see Resources, page 95).

6 IRON WIRE
Uncoated wire, rusted for an aged effect. Available from specialist wire suppliers (see Resources).

7 COAT HANGERS
A cheap, readily available source of thick, hard wire in different colours.

8 MODELLING WIRE
Steel wire with a zigzag shape, manufactured for use in clay sculpting. Available from art suppliers.

9 GARDEN WIRE
Easy-to-manipulate wire, coated with plastic. Ideal for outdoors as well as the kitchen and bathroom, due to its waterproof qualities. Available in a variety of shades and gauges from hardware and gardening stores.

10 FUSE WIRE AND FINE BINDING WIRE
Ideal for binding thicker wire pieces together. Available in a variety of finishes including tinned copper, copper and brass from hardware stores and craft suppliers.

11 SILVER-PLATED JEWELLERY WIRE
Fine, malleable wire with a bright silver finish. Available in a variety of gauges from jewellery, beading and craft suppliers.

12 CHICKEN WIRE
Chicken wire is lightweight and malleable, although protective gloves should be worn when cutting it. Available in various gauges from hardware and gardening stores.

BEADS
13 BEADS
A range of different beads have been used in the projects that involve wire, a perfect medium for threading. When choosing beads, attention should be paid to their hole sizes, making sure that they are compatible with the diameter of the wire used.

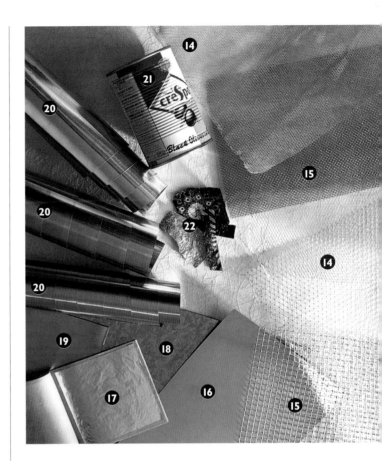

SHEET METAL AND MESH
Sheet metal is produced by passing metal through rollers to produce the desired thickness. As with wire, this thickness is measured in millimetres and/or by a gauge. Sheet meshes come in two forms: the fine, expandable variety, usually made from aluminium, and the harder, solid sort made from steel. Different types within a range are usually defined by the hole sizes, often specified in millimetres or by gauge.

14 EXPANDABLE MESH
Made from aluminium, and extremely soft and pliable. The holes are usually in the shape of a diamond, with different widths depending on the fineness of the mesh. Available from craft and art suppliers or by mail order.

15 HARD MESH
Often made from steel, and very solid and impossible to mould, these meshes are available in various grid patterns and are normally supplied for outdoor domestic purposes. Very fine varieties are possible to mould. Available from hardware stores or by mail order.

16 ALUMINIUM SHEET
Flexible but hardwearing form of sheet metal with a soft, matt silver finish. Available in a variety of gauges, widths and lengths from some hardware stores and specialist metal suppliers.

17 SILVER LEAF
One of the finest forms of sheet metal available, second only to gold. It comes in single sheets, sandwiched for protection between layers of paper. Available in a range of finishes and gauges from art shops and craft suppliers.

18 GALVANIZED STEEL SHEET
Hard, inflexible material with a mottled silver finish, which needs to be cut with specialist tools or by the supplier. Available in a variety of gauges from specialist metal suppliers.

19 PEWTER SHEET
Dull grey, soft sheet metal that is easy to work with. Available from craft suppliers.

20 COPPER, BRASS AND ALUMINIUM FOILS
Usually 0.1–0.2mm thick, these very fine, shiny foils are easy to cut and ideal for embossing. Available in roll form from craft and specialist metal suppliers.

21 TIN CANS
Plain or decorated tin cans are a good source of cheap and decorative sheet metal. Raw tin is sharp, so protective gloves should be worn when working with it.

22 FOIL SWEET WRAPPERS
Plain and decorated foil sweet wrappers are a good way of introducing colour to a design and are inexpensive and readily available.

EQUIPMENT

Most of the equipment used in this book can be found in a basic tool kit or around the home. The more specialist items such as tin snips, round- and bent-nosed pliers, a hole punch and a tracing wheel are available from hardware shops, department stores or craft and metal suppliers. It is important to wear protective gloves and goggles when working with the harder sheet metals, meshes and wires.

23 PLIERS
Useful for gripping and bending metal and wire.

24 ROUND-NOSED PLIERS
Ideal for bending small loops in wire and for finer wirework.

25 BENT-NOSED PLIERS
Useful tool for bending and manipulating wire positioned in awkward places.

26 WIRE CUTTERS
Helpful for cutting wire and finishing ends neatly.

27 GILDER'S TIP
The best tool for picking up and positioning silver leaf without using your hands.

28 WIRE BRUSH
Used for brushing a metal surface to provide an abraded section for gluing purposes.

29 PANEL PINS
Small pins used to pin sections of the softer sheet metals to wood.

30 WET-AND-DRY PAPER
Fine sandpaper used for sanding metal in conjunction with a wooden block.

31 HAND FILE
Used for filing raw edges of metal.

32 WOODEN SPOON
Ideal tool to use when twisting or coiling wire.

33 HAMMER
Used for knocking in panel pins and hammering a centre punch when pattern making.

34 HIDE MALLET
A hammer made from densely rolled leather. It is ideal for gentle hammering as it does not mark metal surfaces.

35 HAND DRILL
Useful tool to help with twisting finer wire.

36 HOLE PUNCH
Quick and effective way of making holes in metal.

37 CENTRE PUNCH
Useful tool for making decorative hole patterns in foil or some harder metals, used in conjunction with a hammer.

38 STAPLE GUN
Ideal tool for securing chicken wire to wood.

39 PROTECTIVE GOGGLES
Wear these when carrying out work on metal and wire where small shards of the material may be produced by cutting or filing or when springy wire is liable to backfire.

40 PROTECTIVE GLOVES
Use when handling raw cut edges of sheet metal, chicken wire and some of the harder meshes.

41 CRAFT KNIFE
Use a sharp craft knife for scoring and cutting some of the sheet metals.

42 TRACING WHEEL
Clever and quick tool for making embossed dotted lines on some of the finer sheet metals.

43 STEEL RULER
Useful for measuring and providing a hard edge for scoring lines in sheet metal.

44 BALLPOINT/MARKER PENS
A ballpoint pen without ink is the perfect tool for drawing embossed designs into fine foils. A permanent marker pen can be used for smudge-free marking.

45 PAIR OF COMPASSES
Useful for drawing out circles on to paper or directly on to metal.

46 MASKING TAPE
Ideal for applying directly to mesh and using as a guide for cutting out a drawn pattern.

47 SCISSORS
Can be used for cutting some of the finer sheet metals and meshes.

48 BENCH VICE
Useful tool for holding the harder sheet metals in place while filing and sanding.

49 TIN SHEARS
Heavy-duty scissors made especially for cutting hard metals.

50 TIN SNIPS
Less 'industrial' than tin shears, these scissors are designed for cutting metals. Good for cutting out smaller shapes and designs.

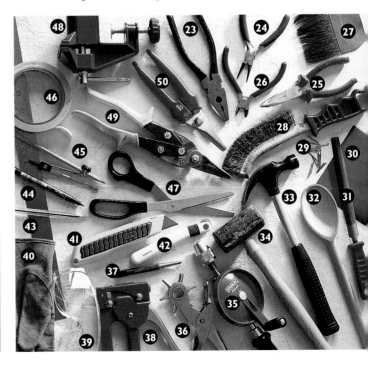

techniques

SAFETY

Metal is a hard material that should be treated with due respect and common sense when you are working with it. Care should be taken to wear protective clothing where appropriate.

It is advisable to wear protective leather gloves and hardy clothing when working with the thicker grade sheet metals such as tin and aluminium.

The same is advised for the tougher wires, particularly chicken wire and the stronger meshes. In some cases (specified in the project instructions), you should wear protective goggles, especially when cutting small lengths of wire or pieces of tin, as these can fly up into your face and cause injury.

Respect should be shown for the tools used to cut metal. These are obviously very powerful and should be kept in a safe place when not in use.

FINISHING RAW EDGES

Care should be taken with raw cut metal edges, particularly tin but also sheet aluminium. To ensure safety, it is best to finish metal by filing down any sharp edges. Always wear protective gloves and goggles when performing this task.

STEP 1 Hold the metal to be filed in place using a holding device such as a bench vice. Take a hand file, place it at right angles to the metal and then file using a forward-moving stroke, easing the pressure as the file is returned. Continue in the same manner until the complete edge has been filed.

STEP 2 Finish off the filed metal edge with wet-and-dry paper so that it is smooth to the touch. The wet-and-dry paper must be dampened first, then wrapped around a cork or wooden block before sanding along the metal edge.

EMBOSSING FOIL

Foil is a delightfully soft material to work with and can be decorated using a variety of techniques. These act to emboss the foil either from the front to achieve an indented effect, or from the back for a raised effect. The decoration can be done freehand or over a paper template.

USING A BALLPOINT PEN

One of the easiest and most effective ways to emboss your design is with an empty ballpoint pen. Simply draw freehand or follow the design on a paper template secured over the foil with masking tape. For the best results, carry out the embossing on top of a 'giving' surface such as a telephone directory.

USING A CENTRE PUNCH

A centre punch can be used to create an indented, pierced dot pattern on your chosen design that can also be reversed for a raised effect. First transfer your design on to paper and secure it in place on the foil with masking tape. Place the foil on top of a piece of wood to protect your work surface. Position the centre punch on the design and hammer once directly on top of the punch for each dot, working your way around the design to complete it.

EMBOSSED EFFECTS

These freehand heart designs show the difference in the indented and raised effects.

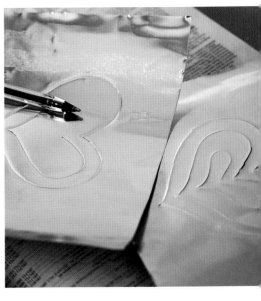

USING A TRACING WHEEL

A tracing wheel, which can be purchased in haberdashery departments, is an ideal tool for quickly and effectively decorating foil with a line or curve of tiny dots. Simply press down as if the wheel were a pencil and follow the design. For straight lines, use a metal ruler as a guide. Again, do this on a telephone directory for the best results.

TEMPLATES ON MESH

It is difficult to cut accurately around a paper template taped on the malleable meshes used in some of the designs. A good tip for achieving extra precision is to transfer your design to a 'sheet' of masking tape.

STEP 1 Take the piece of mesh and lay strips of masking tape side by side to form a sheet of tape, on to which you can transfer your design by pencil.

STEP 2 Cut out the shape following the pencil lines for a neat finish. Remove the masking tape.

MAKING A COILED EDGE

Wire coils flattened out to form a loop design make a useful decorative edging for a variety of projects. They work particularly well when used to finish off and disguise a bound edge, as in the celebration cake and rusted wire cupboard (see pages 16 and 50).

STEP 1 Wrap the wire around a rounded implement, such as the handle of a wooden spoon, a pencil or a broom handle. The diameter of the implement will determine how large the loops will end up. As you wrap, push the wire together several times. Continue winding, depending on how long you wish your loop edging to be.

STEP 2 Ease the wrapped wire off the implement and start to stretch it out. Flatten the loops with your thumb and forefinger as you go along. The loops can overlap each other slightly or sit apart, making individual loops.

MAKING SPIRALS

Spirals are another popular form of decoration in wirework. They can be made loose and open or tightly bound together. They can also be made to follow two different directions from the same piece of wire, as in the wire-spiral jar (see page 48), or bound facing each other and back to back, as in the rusted wire cupboard (see page 50).

OPEN SPIRAL

First make a loop at the beginning of the wire using small pliers. Using your thumb and forefinger, carefully wind the wire around this loop, keeping the wire at a set distance from the loop and maintaining this distance as you continue to wind the wire to form the spiral.

CLOSED SPIRAL

Again make a loop at the beginning of the wire using small pliers. Using your thumb and forefinger, wind the wire tightly around the loop so that the wire touches the loop. Keep winding the wire in this way, using pressure to force the wire to form the tight coil.

SPRING SPIRAL

A spring spiral can be made by wrapping wire around a conical object such as an aperitif glass. Wire of a good strength, say 0.5mm, needs to be used for this method.

STEP 1 Leave a length of 3cm (1¼in) before holding the beginning of the wire firmly in place at the base of the cone with your thumb. Then start to wrap the wire around the cone, leaving a set distance between the turns of the wire.

STEP 2 Cut off the wire at the wider end of the cone where it wraps around to meet itself and remove it from the cone. Make a tight loop at the top of the spiral. For pretty Christmas decorations, thread with frosted and crystal beads to finish the spring spiral.

TWISTING WIRE

Twisted wire is often used in wirework designs and making it is a simple but essential technique to learn. It serves three main purposes: strengthening wire, while at the same time adding flexibility and introducing decoration. There are two methods, and both require the wire to be secured around a steadfast object such as a door handle or banister.

FOR TOUGHER WIRE

This method uses a wooden spoon. Cut the wire to three times your desired finished length. Bend the wire in half and loop the bent section around a door handle or bring it around a banister. Take a wooden spoon and twist the cut ends around the handle several times in an anti-clockwise direction. Hold the wooden spoon so that the wire is horizontal to the handle or banister and pull taut. Begin to wind the spoon in a clockwise direction to create the twist. Continue winding to achieve your required twist (the more you wind, the tighter the twist, and vice versa), holding the wire taut and horizontal to keep the twist even. Stop winding and then, holding the wire instead of the wooden spoon, let the tension release in the wire. Trim the ends with wire cutters.

FOR FINER WIRE

This method uses a hand drill. Cut the wire to double your desired finished length. Bend the wire in half and secure it around a door handle or banister, as with the tougher wire. Take the two cut ends, bind them with masking tape and secure them tightly in the chuck of a hand drill. Keeping the wire horizontal and taut, turn the drill to twist the wire. Release the wire from the chuck and trim the ends with wire cutters.

SAFETY NOTE

Twisting the tougher wires can be dangerous and in this case it is advisable to wear protective goggles and clothing. Because of the pressure used, letting go of the wires too early can cause them to backfire in an uncontrolled manner, accidentally causing injury.

METALLIC PAINTS

Metallic finishes are becoming very fashionable and as a result there is now an enormous variety of metallic paints, waxes and powders on the market. The larger paint companies have become aware of the demand and are now supplying metallic paints at affordable prices in larger pot sizes. Specialist paint and art shops have always been good sources of supply, but they, too, are extending their ranges to incorporate wonderful colours and iridescents, as well as the traditional shades of gold, silver and copper.

Spray-paints in traditional gold, silver and bronze are readily available from good DIY stores and art shops.

Unusual and striking colours such as purple, green, pink, and lustrous opalescents are among the range of new metallic paints now on the market.

templates

butterfly wind-chimes
shown actual size

wire-mesh food covers
shown actual size

EXTEND
TO FIT

EXTEND
TO FIT

monogram wreath

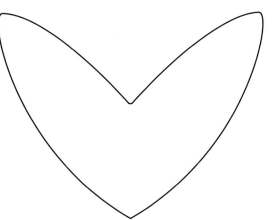

shown actual size

AAABBCCDD EFGHIJKKK LMMNNOPP QQQRRSSTT VVUWWXXY YYZÆ

enlarge as required

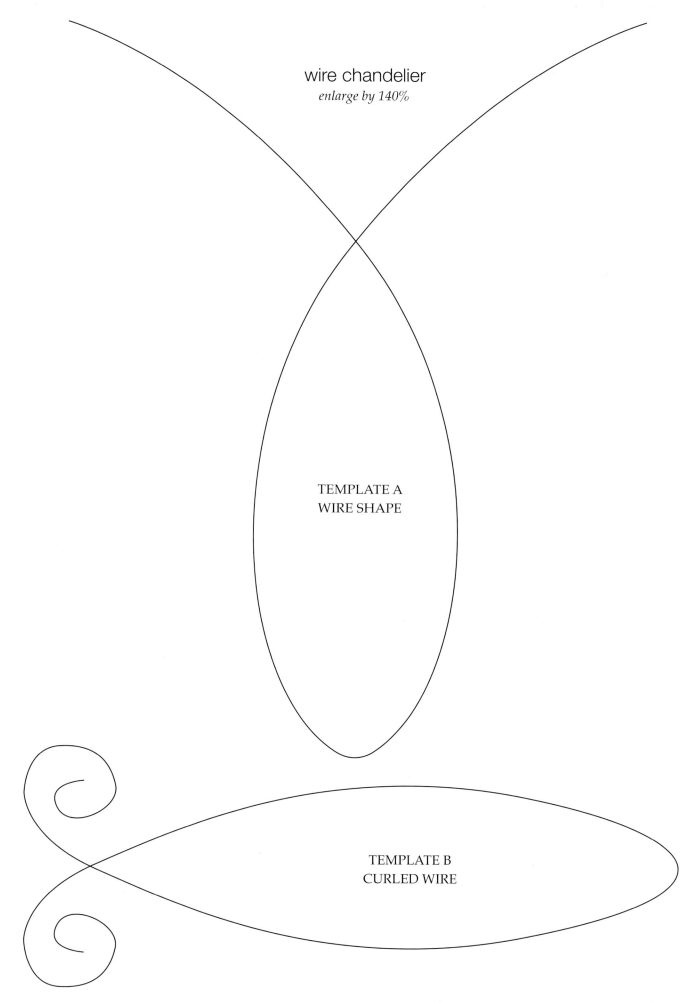

wire chandelier
enlarge by 140%

TEMPLATE A
WIRE SHAPE

TEMPLATE B
CURLED WIRE

resources

UK

Fred Aldous
37 Lever Street
Manchester
M1 1LW
Order line: 08707 517 301
Helpline: 08707 517 300
Website: www.fredaldous.co.uk
Craft suppliers of foils, pewter sheet and wires. Mail order service.

Cornelissen & Son
105 Great Russell Street
London WC1B 3RY
Tel: 020 7636 1045
Metal leaf, powders and associated gilder's tools. Mail order service.

George King
224 Tooting High Street
SW17 OSQ
Tel: 020 8672 8538
Sheet metal (including galvanized steel), foils and wires.

The London Graphic Centre
16–18 Shelton Street
WC2H 9JL
Tel: 020 7759 4500
Website: www.londongraphics.co.uk
Art and craft suppliers of expandable wire mesh and modelling wire.

The Scientific Wire Company
18 Raven Road
London E18 1HW
Tel: 020 8505 0002
Website: www.wires.co.uk
Specialist wires (including 3.25mm aluminium wire and 0.56mm iron wire for rusting). Mail order service available.

J. Smith and Son
42–56 Tottenham Court Road
London N1 4BZ
Tel: 020 7253 1277
Sheet metal, foils and wires.

Alec Tiranti Ltd
27 Warren Street
London W1T 5NB
Tel: 020 7380 0808
Website: www.tiranti.co.uk
Foils and wires.

US

Home Depot, U.S.A., Inc.
2455 Paces Ferry Road
Atlanta, GA 30339-4024
Tel: (770) 433-8211
Website: www.homedepot.com
Home improvement store with more than 1000 locations in the US and Canada. Check Store Locator on the website for the nearest.

Paragona Art Products
1150 18th Street, Suite 200
Santa Monica, CA 90403
Tel: (310) 264-1980 or (800) 991 5899
Supplier of soft copper, brass, pewter and aluminum foil.

American Metalcraft, Inc.
2074 George Street
Melrose Park, IL, 60160-1515
Orders: (800) 333-9133
Customer Service: (708) 345-1177
Website: www.amnow.com
Request a catalog by phone or e-mail info@amnow.com.
Hobby products include: aluminum, copper, brass, bronze, stainless steel, foil, copper tape, tubing, and more.

Craft-Supplies-Online.com
PO Box 4221,
Shawnee Mission,
KS 66204
Tel: (800) 999 9513
Assorted craft supplies.

www.jerrysartarama.com
Aluminium modellimg mesh.

acknowledgments

I would like to thank the contributors who made the projects, without whom this book would not have been possible: Marion Elliot (tin splashback); Emma Hardy (wire-mesh food covers); Jayne Keeley (candy-wrapper mirror frame and wire-handled lanterns and paperweight); Alison Jenkins (wire chandelier, curtain-pole finials and holdbacks, and panelled wardrobe); Deborah Schneebeli Morrell (fairy-light sphere, rusted-wire cupboard, monogram wreath and butterfly wind-chimes); Lesley Stanfield (celebration cake and greetings cards, and Easter egg ornaments).

I would also like to thank photographers Lucinda Symons and Brian Hatton, plus assistants Emma and Holly, for all their hard work and creativity, and my commissioning editor Lindsay Porter and art director Ali Myer at David & Charles for all their help along the way.

Finally, I would like to thank the following UK shops for lending items for photography:
The Pier (Tel: 020 7814 5020)
Damask (Tel: 020 7731 3553)
C.P. Hart (Tel: 020 7902 1000)
Next Home (Tel: 0870 243 5435)

about the author

Lisa Brown is a talented journalist and stylist specializing in home crafts and interiors. Her work has appeared in magazines including *Inspirations*, *BBC Good Homes*, *Ideal Home* and *House Beautiful*. She spent many years as Home Editor of *Inspirations* magazine. Lisa lives in London.

index

adhesive, epoxy resin 73
  metal 27
aluminium
  foil 76, 84, 87
  mesh 7, 8, 14, 18–19, 22–3, 26,
    83, 88
  sheet 7, 64, 72, 84
  wire 8, 58–9, 82

ballpoint pen 64, 85, 87
beaded net 46–7
beads 27, 37–9, 42–3, 46–9, 65, 83
bent-nosed pliers 52, 65, 84
birthday card 14–15
brush, wire 73, 84
butterfly wind-chimes 62–5
  template 92

cake, celebration 16–19
candy-wrapper mirror frame 66–9
centre punch 85, 87
chandelier 34–9
  template 94
chicken wire 30, 52, 83
Christmas light sphere 56–9
coils, making 19, 54, 88
compasses, pair of 18, 85
craft knife 15, 85
cupboard, rusted wire 50–55
curtain-pole finials 40–43

découpage 68–9
doorstop 49
drill 65, 85, 90

earring hooks 39
Easter ornaments 20–23
embossing foil 87
etching spray 36

file, hand 84, 86
finishing raw edges 86
flat-nosed pliers 15, 26
florist's wire 48, 82
foil 7, 60–73, 76, 84, 87
food cover 24–7
  template 92
fuse wire 18, 26, 83

galvanized steel sheet 84
  wire 27, 36, 39, 42, 48,
    65, 72

glass nuggets 43
gloves, protective 18, 22, 26, 30,
  52, 76, 85, 86
goggles, protective 30, 36, 42, 52,
  85, 86
greetings cards 12–15

hammer 76, 85
hand drill 65, 85
  file 84
hide mallet 77, 85
holdbacks, curtain 40–43
hole punch 26, 65, 85

jewellery pliers 39, 42–3
  wire 15, 19, 37–8, 42–2, 46–7, 83

lanterns, wire-handled 44–8

mallet, hide 77, 85
marker pen, permanent 18, 22, 26,
  72, 85
masking tape 59, 72, 85, 88
medium-density fiberboard (MDF)
  53, 68, 76
mesh
  aluminium 7, 8, 14, 18–19, 26,
    83, 88
  steel 26, 83
  wire 7, 8, 14, 18–19, 22–3
metallic spray paint 36, 58, 91
mirror frame 66–9
modelling wire 18, 83
monogram wreath 70–3
  template 93

paints, metallic 36, 58, 91
panel pins 76, 84
panelled wardrobe 28–31
paperweight 48
pewter sheet 26, 84
pipe cleaners 27, 82
pliers
  bent-nosed 52, 65, 84
  flat nosed 15, 26
  jewellery 39, 42–3
  round-nosed 15, 37, 84

ribbon, wire edged 14
round-nosed pliers 15, 37, 84
ruler, steel 68, 78, 85
rusted wire cupboard 51–5

safety 86
scissors
  heavy duty 14, 18, 22, 85
  paper edging 14
sheet
  aluminium 7, 64, 72, 84
  galvanized steel 84
  pewter 26, 84
shellac 69
spirals, wire 48, 89
splashback 74–9
split ring 39
spoon, wooden 54, 65, 85, 88
staple gun 31, 85
steel mesh 26, 83
superglue 19, 23

templates 88, 92–4
tin 7
  cans 76, 84
  shears 76, 85
  snips 85
  splashback 74–9
tracing wheel 64, 73, 85, 87
twisted wire 52, 65, 72
  making 90

vice, bench 85

wardrobe, panelled 28–31
wet-and-dry paper 84, 86
wind-chimes 62–5
wire 7, 82–3
  aluminium 8, 58–9, 82
  chicken 30, 52, 83
  florist's 48, 82
  fuse 18, 26, 83
  galvanized 27, 36, 39, 42, 48, 65, 72
  modelling 18, 83
  rusted 51–5, 83
  silver plated jewellery 15, 19,
    37–8, 42–3, 46–7, 83
  twisted 52, 65, 72
wire brush 73, 84
wire cutters 18, 30, 48, 52, 72, 84
wire-edged ribbon 14
wire mesh 7, 8, 14, 18–19, 22–3
wire spirals 48, 89
wooden spoon 54, 65, 85, 88
wreath 70–3